KETO CHAFFLE COOK WITH PICTURES FOR BEGINNERS 2021

Easy, Low-Carb, Delicious, Gluten-Free Recipes with Pictures to Live a Healthy Life

LORYS ALLEN

DISCLAIMER

TABLE OF CONTENT

Introduction

Chaffles are made using cheese and eggs. Cheese+ waffles make chaffles. Crazy as they sound, they're amazingly easy to make. Eggs and cheese are the principal ingredients, and they hold together shockingly well on a waffle iron.

Use them as a treat, or have them for two or three times each week. All things considered, there's nothing in the recipes you can't eat on a low-carb diet. These are a wonderful method to feel like you're having a treat without going astray from your eating regimen by any means. Without a doubt, they might be savory whereas ordinary waffles are sweet, and they may not combine well with maple syrup. Yet, this is as yet significant on the grounds that one of the factors that decide diet achievement is the number of food alternatives you have accessible to you. These special and innovative food sources have begun as a pattern among those after prohibitive diets. Chaffles contain no flour, which means they are on low carb keto diet. They have become so main stream that even the individuals who aren't on the keto diet need to attempt them as well. They contain cheese which has the ideal macronutrient structure in case you're on a low-carb diet. It's loaded with muscle-building proteins and satisfying fats, and has for all intents and purposes no carbs. Cheese is produced using whey protein, perhaps the best sort of protein you can eat after an exercise to help fix muscle tissue. What's more, one egg likewise contains in excess of 6 grams of protein, making these the most protein-pressed waffles you're truly going to eat. Also, in case you're attempting to remain low-carb on a careful spending plan, they're the most reasonable protein source you will discover. You can eat them as sweet treats, as a morning meal supper or as a bite. Chaffles are alive and well food varieties that follow the ketogenic diet suggestions. They are high-fat, high-protein, and low-starch food sources that can tell the body the best way to utilize fat as an elective fuel to create energy and consume fat.

In this book I will examine chaffles and clarify how they are unique in relation to waffles. I'll clarify the various sorts of chaffles you can undoubtedly make at home. I will likewise dive deep into the ketogenic count calories and talk about its numerous advantages.

These are the things that you will discover in this book

- Health advantages of the ketogenic diet

- Carb count and chaffle nutrition
- Most delicious chaffle recipes

At long last, I will likewise be sharing numerous delectable Keto Chaffle recipes that are altogether simple to get ready. For every recipe, I will give a rundown of ingredients and point by point bit by bit instructions. I'm sure you will discover this book extremely valuable. Enjoy reading delicious recipes!

What Is Ketogenic Diet and Its Benefits

The keto or ketogenic diet recommends eating high-fat, low-carb foods that provide us with healthy fats, proteins, and fewer carbohydrates. The calories we consume come mainly from fats (70%), proteins (20%) and carbohydrates (10%). The diet usually does not count calories. Carbohydrates are counted and limited instead.

The human body converts carbohydrates into glucose to produce energy. Fats, which can also be used to make energy, are largely ignored, which is why it is deposited and we are chased. The ketogenic diet limits carbohydrate intake and stimulates the body to burn fat for energy. For this reason, the ketogenic diet is considered to be very efficient for weight loss.

Even if you eat fewer carbohydrates, the insulin level in the abdomen goes down, so that there is less glucose.

Ketogenic Diet Health Benefits

Not just weight loss, the keto diet helps us in many ways -

- Blood Sugar - It can help us lower blood sugar and insulin levels. A low-carbohydrate diet also prevents spikes in blood sugar.
- Cholesterol - It increases the level of healthy HDL cholesterol and lowers the unhealthy LDL cholesterol. So, it reduces the risk of heart disease.
- The Human Brain - Studies have shown that low-carb, high-protein, and fatty foods make our brains more efficient. It can prevent or slow down Alzheimer's disease, dementia, autism and other similar cognitive diseases.
- Inflammation - Inflammation improves immunity, but chronic inflammation can cause health problems. The keto diet decreases free radical production and controls the negative effects of too much inflammation such as arthritis, eczema and psoriasis.
- Stomach Health - A low-carb diet provides relief from heartburn and acid reflux. It can combat the main problems such as bacterial problems and autoimmune reactions. It also improves digestion.
- Anti-aging - According to research results, the ketogenic diet can also promote longevity.
- Improves Energy - The diet stabilizes insulin levels and provides more energy to the brain and tissues. It also improves slow sleep patterns and decreases REM (Rapid Eye Movement) or superficial sleep.

- PCOS - Carbohydrate-rich foods are not recommended for people suffering from PCOS or polycystic ovary syndrome. Studies have shown that keto foods can improve PCOS markers.
- Triglycerides - Triglyceride levels in the blood can skyrocket if we consume too many carbohydrates, leading to an increased risk of heart disease. Reduce consumption and there is a drastic drop in the level.

Apart from the ones mentioned above, the ketogenic diet can also help us control uric acid levels, improve the health of our eyes, and prevent acne breakouts.

Foods that are allowed and not allowed in the keto diet

What you can eat -
1. Seafood, including sardines, salmon, shrimp, crabs, and tuna. Fatty fish such as sardines and salmon are particularly good.
2. Fresh leafy greens, including broccoli, kale, spinach, cauliflower, turnips, cucumber, lettuce, asparagus, bell pepper.
3. Dairy products, including yogurt and cheese. Avoid flavored yogurt.
4. Meat, including pork, lamb, beef, chicken, and turkey, is allowed.
5. Eggs are rich in protein and are allowed in the keto diet.
6. You can eat nuts and seeds in moderation. Avoid cashews.
7. Tea and coffee are both allowed, but without sugar.
8. Use coconut oil for frying and sautéing.
9. You can have dark chocolate with 80% cocoa.

Foods to avoid -
1. Limit the intake of fruits because most of them contain too much sugar.
2. Most grains are high in sugar and are best avoided.
3. White starches only add empty calories.
4. Beans and legumes are high in carbohydrates.
5. Limit the intake of alcohol and honey.

Cinnamon Cream Cheese Chaffle

Servings: 6 Cook time: 15 min

INGREDIENTS

- 50g /1/4 Cup) Cream Cheese
- 17g (2Tbsp) Almond Flour
- 12g (1Tbsp) Protein Powder
- 2g (1/2 tsp) Baking Powder
- 1 Egg
- 1/2 Tsp Vanilla Extract
- 2g (1 tsp) Ground Cinnamon
- 4g (1 Tbsp) Sugar Substitute

TRAVEL DIRECTIONS

1. Set up the entirety of your
2. Add an egg, cinnamon and your sugar into the bowl. Using your hand blender, blend all into the featheriness.
3. When your egg, cinnamon and sugar are completely blended, add the remainder of the and blend indeed.
4. Add a couple of drops of vanilla concentrate into the blend and ensure everything is completely joined.

5. When your blend is readied, you can turn on your Dash Mini Maker.
6. Splash your scramble little creator with Extra Virgin Olive Oil, add scoop of the combination, close the cover and stand by until the green light switches off - prepared and heated.
7. When the green light switches off and you see the steam decrease it is asign your Chaffle is prepared.
8. Proceed after the entire of your Chaffles are finished.
9. Serve it as you would typically enjoy waffles.
10. Pour Sugar-Free fluid Honey or Maple Syrup.

Nutrition Information:

- Total Fat 5g, Carbohydrates 1g, Fiber0g, Protein4g

Chaffles Breakfast bowl

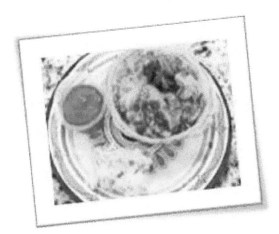

Servings: 2 Cooking time: 5 minutes

INGREDIENTS

- 1 egg
- 1/2 cup cheddar cheese shredded
- pinch of Italian herbs
- 1 tbsp. Pizza sauce
- TOPPING
- 1/2 sliced avocado
- Boiled 2 eggs
- 1 tomato, halved
- 4 oz. fresh spinach leaves

TRAVEL DIRECTIONS

1. Preheat your waffle iron and grease with cooking spray.
2. Break an egg into a bowl and beat with Italian herbs and pizza sauce.
3. Add grated cheese to the egg and herb mixture.
4. Pour 1 tbsp. grated cheese in a waffle iron and cook for 30 sec.
5. Pour Chaffles batter into the waffle iron and close the lid.
6. Bake chaffles for about 4 minutes until crisp and brown.
7. Carefully remove covers from the maker.
8. Serve on the bed of spinach with boiled egg, avocado slice and tomatoes.
9. To enjoy!

Nutritional Information:

- Per Servings: Protein: 23% 77 kcal Fat: 66% 222 kcal Carbohydrates: 11% 39 kcal

Sweet Chaffles

Serving: 1 Cook time: 2 min

INGREDIENTS

- 2 oz Cream Cheese
- 1 Egg
- 1 Tablespoon Coconut Flour
- 2 Teaspoon Cocoa
- 1.5 Tablespoons Sweetener (you can use between 2-3, I prefer 2.5)
- 1 Teaspoons Vanilla
- 1/2 Teaspoon Baking Soda
- 1 Teaspoons Cinnamon which is optional
- Coconut Oil Spray
- Waffle Maker
- 1 Teaspoon Butter

TRAVEL DIRECTIONS

1. Firstly, Place cream cheese into a microwave safe bowl and microwave for 20 seconds. Then Mix the rest of your sweet chaffle in to the bowl with the cream cheese.
2. After this Plug-in your waffle maker and spray with coconut oil.
3. Spoon just enough of your combined sweet chaffle on to the waffle maker.
4. Close your waffle maker and wait patiently, yes - it will be hard.

5. The exact cook time varies, depending on your waffle maker. We find that most waffle makers cook the sweet chaffles in approximately 2 minutes.
6. Remove your cooked sweet chaffle and place on a plate.
7. Top it with a slice of butter.
8. Enjoy!

Nutritional Information:

- Amount Per Serving: CALORIES: 721TOTAL FAT: 54gSATURATED FAT: 30gTRANS FAT: 0gUNSATURATED FAT: 19gCHOLESTEROL: 305mgSODIUM: 668mgCARBOHYDRATES: 39gFIBER: 3gSUGAR: 6gPROTEIN:18g

Keto BLT Chaffle

Servings: 2 Cook time: 3 min

INGREDIENTS

Chaffle
1 Egg (beaten)
1/2 cup Cheddar cheese (grated)
1 tablespoon Almond flour (blanched)
1/2 teaspoon Baking powder
BLT with Avocado
3 strips Bacon (cooked)
1 piece Bibb lettuce
1 slice Tomato (fresh)
1/4 Avocado (thinly sliced)

TRAVEL DIRECTIONS

1. Chaffle
2. Spray mini-waffle maker with cooking spray then preheat untilready.
3. In a small bowl, mixall of the chaffle You can also mix in a blender.
4. Then Pour enough batter into the center of the waffle maker and spread to fill the edges. If you overfill the first one use less each time so you avoid spill over. Close down the lid and allow it to cookfor 3 1/2 minutes.

5. Remove the chaffle and allow to cool on a cooling rack – repeat the process for the second chaffle.
6. BLT with Avocado
7. Then Add a piece of bibb lettuce, a tomato slice, and strips of bacon on a chaffle and top it with the slashed avocado and second chaffle. (If you prefer, a creamy guacamole instead of the avocado would be delicious.
8. Plate and appreciate.

Nutritional Information:
- Serving: 1 sandwich | Calories: 631kcal | Carbohydrates: 5g | Protein: 31g | Fat: 60g | Saturated Fat: 23g | Cholesterol: 267mg | Sodium: 855mg | Potassium: 554mg | Fiber: 2g | Sugar: 2g | Calcium: 447mg | Net Carbs: 3g

Best Pumpkin Chaffle

Serving: 2 Cook Time: 5 min

INGREDIENTS

- 1 medium egg
- 1/3 cup shredded mozzarella cheese
- 1 tablespoon pumpkin
- 1 teaspoon pumpkin pie spice
- 1/4 teaspoon baking powder
- 1-3 teaspoons monk fruit sweetener

Instructions

1. Firstly, mix egg, cheese, pumpkin, spice, baking powder and sweetener in a little bowl.
2. Whisk egg and cheese. Then Cook on mini waffle maker, and enjoy.

Nutrition Information:

Gluten free, low carb

Crazy Good Cinnamon Orange Keto Waffle Recipe

Servings: 2 Cook time: 3 min

INGREDIENTS

- One large egg
- ½ shredded
- 1/2 tsp Grated orange peel
- 1/8 teaspoon ground cinnamon
- Butter & sugar-free

TRAVEL DIRECTIONS

1. Firstly heat up your waffle iron and spray both sides with nonstick cooking spray.
2. Crack your egg and whisk it using use a fork ,a grater or zester to zest about 1/2 teaspoon of orange zest or more if you would like
3. Now add the zest to the whisked egg.
4. Combine in a pinch or 1/8 teaspoon of ground cinnamon

5. Add shredded mozzarella cheese
6. Combine well
7. Place half of the mixture into one side of the waffle iron. This mixture makes 2 regular sized waffles on a waffle iron that makes 4 waffles. So, keep in mind depending on the size and shape of your waffle iron you might need to adjust how you add the batter.
8. The chaffle batter should cover the selected space for 2 waffles.
9. Use your spatula to spread the paste evenly.
10. Close the lid to your waffle iron. Let it cook for about 3 minutes.
11. The chaffle is easy to flip once it has been on the waffle iron for 2-3 minutes. So I turn it and close the lid for 1 minute more.
12. chaffle should be golden brown.

Cream Mini chaffles

Servings: 2 Cooking time: 10 minutes

INGREDIENTS

- 2 tsp coconut flour
- 4 teaspoons swerve / monk fruit
- ¼ tsp baking powder
- 1 egg
- 1 oz cream cheese
- ½ teaspoon of vanilla extract

TRAVEL DIRECTIONS

1. Turn on the waffle iron to heat it up and coat it with cooking spray.
2. In a small mixing bowl, combine swerve / monk fruit, coconut flour and baking powder.
3. Add cream cheese, egg, vanilla extract and beat until well blended.
4. Add the batter to the waffle iron and bake for 3 minutes, until golden brown.
5. Serve with your favorite toppings.

Nutritional Information:

- Carbohydrates: 4 g; Fat: g; Protein: 2 g; Calories: 73

Raspberry Chaffles

Servings: 2 Cooking time: 5 minutes

INGREDIENTS

- 4 tablespoons of almond flour
- 4 large eggs
- 2⅓ cup of grated mozzarella cheese
- 1 teaspoon of vanilla extract
- 1 tablespoon of erythritol sweetener
- 1½ tsp baking powder
- ½ cup of raspberries

TRAVEL DIRECTIONS

1. Turn on the waffle iron to heat it up and coat it with cooking spray.
2. Combine almond flour, sweetener and baking powder in a bowl.
3. Add cheese, eggs and vanilla extract and mix until well blended.
4. Add 1 portion of batter to the waffle iron and spread it evenly. Close and cook for 3 minutes, or until golden brown.
5. Repeat until the remaining batter has been used.
6. Serve with raspberries.

Nutritional Information: Carbohydrates: 5 g; Fat: 11 g; Protein: 24 g; Calories: 300

Protein Mozzarella Chaffles

Servings: 4 Cooking time: 20

INGREDIENTS

- ½ scoop of unsweetened protein powder
- 2 large organic eggs
- ½ cup of mozzarella cheese, shredded
- 1 tablespoon of Erythritol
- ¼ teaspoon of organic vanilla extract

TRAVEL DIRECTIONS

1. Preheat a mini waffle iron and then grease it.
2. Place all in a medium bowl and mix with a fork until well blended.
3. Place ¼ of the mixture in the preheated waffle iron and bake for about 4-5 minutes or until golden brown.
4. Repeat with the remaining mixture.
5. Serve warm.

Nutritional Information: per Portions: Calories: Net carbohydrates: 0.4 g Fat: 3.3 g Saturated fat: 1.2 g Carbohydrates: 0.4 g Dietary fiber: 0 g Sugar: 0.2 g Protein: 7.3 g

Chocolate Chips Peanut Butter Chaffles

Servings: 2 Cooking time: 8 minutes

INGREDIENTS

- 1 organic egg, beaten
- ¼ cup of mozzarella cheese, cut into pieces
- 2 tablespoons of creamy peanut butter
- 1 tablespoon of almond flour
- 1 tablespoon of granular erythritol
- 1 teaspoon of organic vanilla extract
- 1 tablespoon of 70% dark chocolate chips

TRAVEL DIRECTIONS

1. Preheat a mini waffle iron and then grease it.
2. Place all except chocolate chips in a bowl and beat until well blended.
3. Gently fold in the chocolate chips.
4. Place half of the mixture in the preheated waffle iron and bake for about minutes or until golden brown.
5. Repeat with the remaining mixture.
6. Serve warm.

Nutritional Information: Per Servings:

- Calories: 214 Net Carbs: 4.1g Fat: 16.8g Saturated Fat: 5.4g Carbohydrates: 6.4g Dietary Fiber: 2.3g Sugar: 2.1g Protein: 8.8 g

Grain-Free, Low-Carb Keto Waffles

Serving: 2 Cook time: 15 min

INGREDIENTS

- tablespoon of almond flour
- 1 egg
- 1 teaspoon vanilla
- 1 shake of cinnamon
- 1 teaspoon baking powder
- 1 cup mozzarella cheese

TRAVEL DIRECTIONS

1. Firstly, In a bowl, mix together, egg and vanilla extract.
2. Lastly, add in the mozzarella cheese and coat it evenly with the mixture.
3. Spray your waffle maker with oil and let it heat up to its highest setting.
4. Cook the waffle, checking on it every 5 minutes until it gets crunchy and golden. A tip: Make sure you put in half of your batter. The waffle maker can overflow, making it a messy process. I suggest putting down a silpat mat for an easy clean up.
5. Take it out carefully, and top it with butter, and your favorite low-carb syrup.

NUTRITIONAL INFORMATION:

Calories per serving: 127 Kcal ; Fat: 10 g ; Carbohydrates: 5.5 g ; Protein: 7 g

Low-Carb Caramel Chaffle

Servings: 2 Cook time:10 min

INGREDIENTS

- Tbsp. Turn confectioners' sugar substitute
- Tbsp. Almond flour
- 1 Egg
- ½ tsp. Vanilla concentrate
- ⅓ C. Destroyed mozzarella cheddar
- For the caramel sauce:
- Tbsp. Margarine unsalted
- 2 Tbsp. Turn brown sugar substitute
- ⅓ C. Weighty whipping cream

TRAVEL DIRECTIONS

1. Preheat your scaled down waffle producer.
2. Spot the 3 tablespoons of margarine and the 2 tablespoons of earthy colored sugar substitute together in a little skillet or dish over medium warmth on the oven.
3. Cook the margarine and sugar substitute combination for 4-5 minutes until it starts to brown however not consume.
4. Add the weighty whipping cream into the combination on the oven, and whisk it in well. Cook the combination on a low bubble for 10

minutes until the blend thickens and has the shade of caramel sauce.

5. While the caramel sauce is cooking, combine as one the elements for the chaffles in a blending bowl.
6. Spot half of the chaffle combination into the warmed small scale waffle producer, and cook for 3-5 minutes until your ideal degree ofdoneness has been reached.

7. Eliminate the first chaffle, and cook the second 50% of the hitter for another 3-5 minutes.
8. Take the polished caramel sauce off the warmth, and include the vanilla concentrate. Let cool somewhat.
9. Pour the caramel sauce over the chaffles and serve.

NUTRITION INFORMATION:

- 2 carbs

Strawberry Shortcake Chaffles

Servings: 1 Cook time: 10 min

INGREDIENTS

- egg
- 1/3 cup shredded mozzarella cheese
- 1 tbsp almond flour
- 1 tbsp cream cheese
- 1/2 tbsp Swerve (or any low carb sweetener)
- 1/4 tsp baking powder
- 3-4 sliced strawberries
- Whipped Cream
- 1 cup heavy whipping cream
- 1 tbsp Swerve
- 1/2 tsp vanilla extract

TRAVEL DIRECTIONS

1. Firstly, preheat your mini waffle maker. Combine all of your chaffle together in a small bowl (egg, mozzarella, almond flour, cream cheese, low carb sweetener and baking powder). Grease your waffle maker with a non-stick spray and pour half of the batter in. Cook until the automatic timer or light goes off; repeat for next

waffle.

2. While the chaffles are cooling, whip the heavying whipping cream, low carb sweetener and vanilla extract together with a hand mixer until stiff peaks form (this takes about 5 minutes). *See Notes Below

3. Layer the sweet chaffles, whipped cream and sliced strawberries together. Appreciate!

Nutritional Information:
- Calories: 153 Net Carbs: 2g Fat: 12.3g Saturated Fat: 2g Carbohydrates: 3. Dietary Fiber: 1.6g Sugar: 1.2g Protein: 7.9g

Pumpkin Chaffles

Servings: 2 Cooking time: 12 minutes

INGREDIENTS

- 1 organic egg, beaten
- ½ cup of mozzarella cheese, shredded
- 1½ tablespoons of homemade pumpkin puree
- ½ teaspoon of Erythritol
- ½ teaspoon of organic vanilla extract
- ¼ teaspoon pumpkin pie spice

TRAVEL DIRECTIONS

1. Preheat a mini waffle iron and then grease it.
2. Put all in a bowl and beat until well blended.
3. Place ¼ of the mixture in the preheated waffle iron and bake for about 4-6 minutes or until golden brown.
4. Repeat with the remaining mixture.
5. Serve warm.

Nutritional Information:

- Calories: 59 Net Carbs: 1.2g Fat: 3.5g Saturated Fat: 1.5g Carbohydrates: 1 Dietary Fiber: 0.4g Sugar: 0.7g Protein: 4.9 g

Bacon & Jalapeño Chaffles

Servings: 5 Cooking time: 15 minutes

INGREDIENTS

- 3 tablespoons of coconut flour
- 1 teaspoon of organic baking powder
- ¼ teaspoon of salt
- ½ cup of cream cheese, softened
- 3 large organic eggs
- 1 cup of crisp Cheddar cheese, shredded
- 1 jalapeño pepper, seeded and cut into pieces
- 3 slices of bacon cooked, crumbled

TRAVEL DIRECTIONS

1. Heat a mini waffle iron and grease it then.
2. Place the flour, baking powder and salt in a small bowl and mix well.
3. Put the cream cheese in a large bowl and beat until light and fluffy.
4. Add the eggs and Cheddar cheese and beat until well blended.
5. Add the flour mixture and beat until combined.
6. Fold in the jalapeño pepper.

7. Divide the mixture into 5 portions.
8. Place 1 serving of the mixture in the preheated waffle iron and bake for about 5 minutes or until golden brown.
9. Repeat with the remaining mixture.
10. Serve hot with the bacon topping.

Nutritional Information:

- Calories: 249 Net Carbs: 2.9g Fat: 20.3g Saturated Fat: 5g Carbohydrates: 4.8g Dietary Fiber: 1.9g Sugar: 0.5g Protein: 12, 7 g

Acocado Chaffle Toast

Servings: 2 Cooking time: 8 minutes

INGREDIENTS

- ½ Avoca do
- 1 egg
- ½ cup of cheddar cheese, chopped
- 1 tbsp almond flour
- 1 teaspoon lemon juice, fresh
- Salt, ground pepper to taste
- Parmesan cheese, finely chopped for garnish

TRAVEL DIRECTIONS

1. Heat up your mini waffle iron.
2. In a small bowl, mix the egg, almond flour and cheese.
3. For a crispy crust, add a teaspoon of grated cheese to the waffle iron and cook for seconds.
4. Then pour the mixture into the waffle iron and cook for 5 minutes or until crispy.
5. Repeat with the remaining batter.
6. Puree avocado with a fork until well blended and add lemon juice, salt and pepper
7. Cover each chaffle with avocado mixture. Sprinkle with

Parmesan and enjoy!

Nutritional Information:

- Calories per serving: 250 Kcal ; Fat: 23 g ; Carbohydrates: 9 g ;
  Protein: 14 g

Broccoli Chaffles with 3 cheese

Servi ngs: 4 Cooking time: 16 minutes

INGREDIENTS

- ½ cup of cooked broccoli, finely chopped
- 2 organic eggs, beaten
- ½ cup of cheddar cheese, shredded
- ½ cup of mozzarella cheese, shredded
- 2 tablespoons Parmesan cheese, grated
- ½ teaspoon of onion powder

TRAVEL DIRECTIONS

1. Preheat a waffle iron and then grease it.
2. Put all in a bowl and mix until well blended.
3. Place half of the mixture in the preheated waffle iron and bake for about 4 minutes or until golden brown.
4. Repeat with the remaining mix.
5. Serve warm.

Nutritional Information:

- Calories: 112 Net Carbs: 1.2g Fat: 8.1g Saturated Fat: 4.3g Carbohydrates: 1.5g Dietary Fiber: 0.3g Sugar: 0.5g Protein: 8.

Bacon And Ham Chaffle Sandwich

Servings: 2 Cooking time: 5 minutes

INGREDIENTS

- 3 eggs
- ½ cup of grated Cheddar cheese
- 1 tablespoon of almond flour
- ½ tsp baking powder
- For the toppings:
- 4 strips of cooked bacon
- 2 pieces of Bibb lettuce
- 2 slices preferably ham
- 2 slices of tomato

TRAVEL DIRECTIONS

1. Turn on the waffle iron to heat it up and coat it with cooking spray.
2. Combine all of the chaffle components in a small bowl.
3. Add about 1/4 of the total batter to the waffle iron and spread to fill the edges. Cover and cook for 4 minutes.
4. Remove and cool on a rack.
5. Repeat for the second chaffle.
6. Place a slice of tomato, a piece of lettuce and strips of bacon on ahusk, and cover with a second husk.
7. Plate and enjoy.

Nutritional Information:

- Carbohydrates: 5 g; Fat: 60 g; Protein: 31 g; Calories: 631

Ham and Jalapenos Chaffle

Servings: 3 Cooking time: 9 minutes

INGREDIENTS

- 2 l bs cheddar cheese, finely grated
- 2 large eggs
- ½ jalapeno pepper, finely grated
- 2 ounces of ham steak
- 1 medium spring onion
- 2 tsp coconut flour

TRAVEL DIRECTIONS

1. Spray your waffle iron with cooking spray and heat for 3 minutes.
2. Pour 1/4 of the batter mixture into the waffle iron.
3. Cook for 3 minutes, until crispy on the edges.
4. Remove the waffles from the heat and repeat until all the batter is cooked.
5. Once done, let them cool to room temperature and enjoy.

6. Chop the cheddar cheese with a fine grater.
7. Remove the seeds from the jalapeno and grate with the same grater.
8. Finely chop the spring onion and ham.
9. Pour all of it

Nutritional Information:

- Calories per serving: 120 Kcal ; Fat: 10g ; Carbohydrates: 2g ; Protein: 12

Burger Chaffle

Servings: 1 Cooking time: 10 minutes

INGREDIENTS:

- For the cheeseburgers:
- 1/3-pound beef, ground
- ½ tsp garlic salt
- 3 slices of American cheese
- For the Chaffles:
- 1 large egg
- ½ cup of mozzarella, chopped finely
- Salt and ground pepper to taste
- For the Big Mac Sauce:
- 2 tsp mayonnaise
- 1 teaspoon of ketchup
- Collect:
- 2 tablespoons of lettuce, cut into strips
- 4 pickles with dill
- 2 tsp onion, finely chopped
- To assemble burgers:

TRAVEL DIRECTIONS

1. Take your burger patties and put them on a chaffle. Top with shredded lettuce, onions, and pickles.

2. Divide the sauce over the other chaffle and place it on top of the vegetables, sauce side down.

3. To enjoy.

Nutritional Information:

- Calories per serving: 850 Kcal ; Fat: 56 g ; Carbohydrates: 8 g ; Protein: 67 g

Chaffles With Topping

Servings: 3 Cooking time: 10 minutes

INGREDIENTS

- 1 large egg
- 1 tbsp. almond flour
- 1 tbsp. full-fat Greek yogurt
- 1/8 teaspoon of baking powder
- 1/4 cup of grated Swiss cheese
- TOPPING
- 4 oz. grill shrimp
- 4 oz. steamed cauliflower puree
- 1/2 zucchini sliced
- 3 salad leaves
- 1 tomato, sliced
- 1 tbsp. linseed

TRAVEL DIRECTIONS

1. Make 3 chaffles with the given chaffles
2. Before serving, arrange the salad leaves on each chaffle.
3. Top with zucchini slice, grill shrimp, cauliflower puree, and a

tomato slice.

4. Drizzle flaxseed on top.

5. Serve and enjoy!

Nutritional Information:

- Per Servings: Protein: 45% 71 kcal Fat: 47% 75 kcal Carbohydrates:8% 12 kcal

Chaffle With Cheese & Bacon

Servings: 2 Cooking time: 15 minutes

INGREDIENTS

- 1 egg
- 1/2 cup of cheddar cheese, shredded
- 1 tbsp. p poor cheese
- 3/4 teaspoon of coconut flour
- 1/4 teaspoon baking powder
- 1/8 teaspoon of Italian seasoning
- pinch of salt
- 1/4 teaspoon of garlic powder
- FOR TOPPING
- 1 bacon sliced, cooked and chopped
- 1/2 cup mozzarella cheese, shredded
- 1/4 teaspoon parsley, chopped

TRAVEL DIRECTIONS

1. Preh eat the oven at 400 degrees.
2. Turn on your waffle iron and coat with cooking spray.
3. Mix chaffle in a mixing bowl until combined.
4. Spoon half of the batter into the center of the waffle iron and close the lid. Cook chaffles in about 3 minutes.
5. Carefully remove chaffles from the maker.
6. Place the husks on a greased baking tray.

7. Top with mozzarella cheese, chopped bacon, and parsley.
8. And bake in the oven for 4-5 minutes.
9. Once the cheese has melted, remove it from the oven.
10. Serve and enjoy!

Nutritional Information:
- Per Servings: Protein: 28% 90 kcal Fat: 69% 222 kcal Carbohydrates: 3% kcal

Crispy Fish And Chaffle Bites

Servings: 4 Cooking time: 15 minutes

INGREDIENTS

- 1 pound cod fillets, cut into 4 slices
- 1 tsp. sea salt
- 1 tsp. g arlic powder
- 1 egg, beaten
- 1 cup of almond flour
- 2 tablespoons. avocado oil
- CHAFFLE
- 2 eggs
- 1/2 cup of cheddar cheese
- 2 tablespoons. almond flour
- ½ tsp. Italian spices

TRAVEL DIRECTIONS

1. Mix the of the chaffle in a bowl and make 4 squares
2. Place the chaffles in a preheated chaffle maker.
3. Combine the salt, pepper and garlic powder in a mixing bowl. Toss the cod cubes through this mixture and let stand for 10 minutes.
4. Then dip each slice of cod in the egg mixture and then in the almond flour.
5. Heat oil in a skillet and fish cubes for about 2-3 minutes, until

cooked and brown

6. Serve on chaffles and enjoy!

Nutritional Information:

- Per Servings: Protein: 38% 121 kcal Fat: 59% 189 kcal Carbohydrates: 3% 11 kcal

Chaffle Minutesi Sandwich

Servings: 2 Cooking time: 10 minutes

INGREDIENTS

- 1 large egg
- 1/8 cup of almond flour
- 1/2 tsp. garlic powder
- 3/4 tsp. baking powder
- 1/2 cup of grated cheese
- FILL SANDWICH
- 2 slices of deli ham
- 2 slices of tomatoes
- 1 slice of cheddar chee se

TRAVEL DIRECTIONS

1. Grease and preheat your square waffle iron over medium heat.
2. In a mixing bowl, mix the chaffle until well combined.
3. Pour the batter into a square wafer and make two chaffles.
4. When the chaffles are cooked, remove them from the maker .
5. For a sandwich deli, arrange ham, tomato slice and cheddar cheese between two chaffles.
6. Cut sandwich from the center.
7. Serve and enjoy!

Nutritional Information:

- Per Servings: Protein: 29% 70 kcal Fat: 66% 159 kcal Carbohydrates: 4% 10 kcal

Chaffle Cheese Sandwich

Servings: 1 Cooking time: 10 minutes

INGREDIENTS

- 2 square keto chaffle
- 2 slices of cheddar cheese
- 2 salad leaves

TRAVEL DIRECTIONS

1. Prepare your oven for 4000 F.
2. Divide salad leaves and cheese slices between chaffles.
3. Bake in the preheated oven for about 4-5 minutes until the cheese has melted.
4. Once the cheese has melted, remove it from the oven.
5. Serve and enjoy!

Nutritional Information:

- Per Servings: Protein: 28% kcal Fat: 69% 149 kcal Carbohydrates: 3% 6 kcal

Cauliflower Chaffles And Tomatoes

Servings: 2 Cooking time: 15 minutes

INGREDIENTS

- 1/2 cup of cauliflower
- 1/4 tsp. garlic powder
- 1/4 tsp. black pepper
- 1/4 tsp. salt
- 1/2 cup of shredded cheddar cheese
- 1 egg
- FOR TOPPING
- 1 leaf of lettuce
- 1 tomato sliced
- 4 oz. cauliflower steamed, mashed
- 1 teaspoon of sesame seeds

TRAVEL DIRECTIONS

1. Add all the chaffle to a blender and mix well.
2. Sprinkle 1/8 grated cheese on the waffle iron and pour the cauliflower mixture into a preheated waffle iron and sprinkle the restof the cheese on top.
3. Cook chaffles in about 4-5 minutes
4. Before serving, place the lettuce leaves over the chaffle top with steamed cauliflower and tomato.
5. Drizzle over the sesame seeds.
6. To enjoy!

Nutritional Information:

- Per Servings: Protein: 25% 49 kcal Fat: 65% 128 kcal Carbohydrates: 10% 21 kcal

Keto Chaffle Glazed Donut

Servings: 3 Cook time: 10 min

INGREDIENTS

- For the chaffles
- ½ cup Mozzarella cheddar destroyed
- ounce Cream Cheese
- tablespoon Unflavored whey protein disengage
- tablespoon Swerve confectioners sugar substitute
- ½ teaspoon Baking powder
- ½ teaspoon Vanilla concentrate
- 1 Egg
- For the coating besting:
- 2 tablespoon Heavy whipping cream
- 3-4 tablespoon Swerve confectioners sugar substitute
- ½ teaspoon Vanilla concentrate

TRAVEL DIRECTIONS

1. Preheat your smaller than normal waffle creator.
2. In a microwave safe bowl, join the mozzarella cheddar and cream cheddar. Warmth at 30 second stretches until the cheeses are dissolved and totally joined.

3. Add the whey protein, 2 tbsp Swerve confectioners' sugar, preparing powder to the cheddar blend, and massage with your hands until very much fused.

4. Spot the mixture into a blending bowl, and beat the egg and vanilla intoit until a smooth hitter structure.

5. Put 33% of the hitter into the smaller than normal waffle creator, and cook for 3-5 minutes until your ideal degree of doneness has been reached.

6. Rehash stage 5 with the leftover ⅔ of the hitter, for an aggregate of 3 chaffles made.

7. Beat together the elements for the coating besting, and pour over the chaffles prior to serving.

Nutritional Information:

- Net 2 carbs

Easy Keto Choco Chaffle RecipeE

Servings: 2 Cook time: 8 min

INGREDIENTS

- 1/2 cup Sugar-Free Chocolate Chips
- 1/2 cup Butter
- 3 Eggs
- 1/4 cup Truvia, or other sugar
- teaspoon Vanilla concentrate

TRAVEL DIRECTIONS

1. In a microwave safe bowl, dissolve margarine and chocolate for around1 moment. Eliminate and mix well. You truly need to utilize the warmth inside the margarine and chocolate to soften the remainder of the clusters. On the off chance that you microwave until it's completely dissolved, you've overcooked the chocolate. So get a spoon and begin mixing. Add 10 seconds if necessary yet mix a long time before you choose to do that.

2. In a bowl, add eggs, sugar, and vanilla and mix until light and foamy.

3. Pour the liquefied spread and chocolate into the bowl in a sluggish stream and beat again until it is very much fused.

4. Pour around 1/4 of the combination into a Dash Mini Waffle Maker, and cook for 7-8 minutes, or until firm.
5. Should make 4 waffles, with a little bater left finished.

Nutritional Information:

- Calories: 672kcal | Carbohydrates: 11g | Protein: 13g | Fat: 70g | Fiber: 5g | Sugar: 1g

Neapolitan Chaffles

Servings: 2 Cook time: 10 min

INGREDIENTS

- ½ cup mozzarella cheddar shredded
- ounce cream cheddar
- tablespoon almond flour
- tablespoon low carb powdered sugar (I use Lakanto
- 2 tablespoon hefty whipping cream
- 1 enormous egg
- ½ teaspoon vanilla concentrate
- 2-3 medium strawberries mixed or crushed
- 1 tablespoon Cocoa powder unsweetened
- 2 tablespoon Sugar free whipped cream (custom made formula here
- 1-2 tablespoon Sugar free chocolate sauce (I use ChocZero

TRAVEL DIRECTIONS

1. Preheat your small waffle creator.
2. Add the mozzarella and cream cheeses to a microwave safe bowl, and warmth at 30 second stretches until totally liquefied and all around mixed into a cheddar mixture.
3. Add the almond flour and sugar to the cheddar blend, and ply with yourhands until very much consolidated.

4. Spot the mixture into a blending bowl, and include the substantial whipping cream, egg and vanilla concentrate. Mix on high until a smooth hitter has framed.

5. Separate the player into 3 equivalent parts. Leave one segment for whatit's worth, add the pounded strawberries to the subsequent bit, and add the cocoa powder to the third part.

6. Alternate cooking the vanilla, strawberry and chocolate hitters in the little waffle creator until you have three chaffles made.

7. Top the chaffle with sugar free whipped cream and chocolate sauce prior to serving. You can likewise add some extra squashed strawberries to the top whenever wanted.

Nutritional Information:

- 2 SERVING SIZE: 1
- Amount Per Serving: CALORIES: 239TOTAL FAT: 19gSATURATED FAT: 11gTRANS FAT: 0gUNSATURATED FAT: 7gCHOLESTEROL

Chaffles With Keto Ice Cream

Servings: 2 Cooking time: 14 minutes

INGREDIENTS

- 1 egg, beaten
- ½ cup of finely grated mozzarella cheese
- ¼ cup of almond flour
- 2 tablespoons of swapping confectioner's sugar
- 1/8 teaspoon of xanthan gum
- Low-carbohydrate ice cream (flavor of your choice) for serving

TRAVEL DIRECTIONS

1. Preheat the waffle iron.
2. Combine all INGREDIENTS except for the ice cream in a medium bowl.
3. Open the iron and add half of the mixture. Close and cook until crispy, 7 minutes.
4. Place the chaffle on a plate and make a second with the remaining batter.

5. Add a scoop of low-carb ice cream on each chaffle, fold in half moons and enjoy.

Nutritional Information:

- Calories 89 Fat 48g Carbohydrates 1.67g Net Carbohydrates 1.37g Protein 5.91g

Vanilla Mozzarella Chaffles

Servings: 2 cooking time: 12 minutes

INGREDIENTS

- 1 organic egg, beaten
- 1 teaspoon of organic vanilla extract
- 1 tablespoon of almond flour
- 1 teaspoon of organic baking powder
- Pinch of ground cinnamon
- 1 cup mozzarella cheese, shredded

TRAVEL DIRECTIONS

1. Preheat a mini waffle iron and then grease it.
2. Put the egg and vanilla extract in a bowl and beat until well blended.
3. Add the flour, baking powder and cinnamon and mix well.
4. Add the mozzarella cheese and stir to combine.
5. Place the egg and mozzarella cheese in a small bowl and stir to combine.
6. Place half of the mixture in the preheated waffle iron and bake for about 5 minutes or until golden brown.
7. Repeat and eat with the remaining mixture.
8. Serve warm.

Nutritional Information:

- Per Servings: Calories: 103 Net Carbs: 2.4g Fat: 6.6g Saturated Fat: 2.3g Carbohydrates: 2 Dietary Fiber: 0.5g Sugar: 0.6g Protein: 6.8g

Sugar-Free and Keto Smores Chaffle Recipe

Serving: 2 Cook time:10 min

INGREDIENTS

- Marshmallows:

- 100 g, Xylitol

- 40 ml, Water

- 7 g, Gelatine Powder

- Sweet Chaffles:

- 17-gram, Almond Flour

- 12-gram, Protein Powder - Unflavored

- 2 1 gram, Baking powder

- huge, Egg

- 0.50 tsp, Vanilla concentrate
- gram, Ground Cinnamon
- g, Lakanto Sugar Substitute
- 50 g, Cream cheddar
- Chocolate Ganache:
- 80g Sugar-Free Chocolate
- 10g Cacao Butter

TRAVEL DIRECTIONS

1. Using well known Dash Mini Maker, make your Sweet Chaffles ahead of time as the initial phase in our formula.

2. When your Sweet Chaffles are done, you can proceed with Keto Marshmallows, following strides in the formula until you get the ideal cushion out of the blend.

3. Take one of the sweet Chaffle and with a spatula spread the Marshmallow Fluff onto the Chaffle using roundabout Motions. Check the video for a superior agreement.

4. When you are prepared with spreading and content with the thickness of Marshmallows, cover the top with another sweet Chaffle.

5. Delicately press both of the Chaffles against the marshmallow cushion, ensuring Sugar-Free marshmallow is spread equally all through the entirety of the Chaffles from inside. You can even the sides with the edge of the blade to have everything completely even.

6. Let the entirety of the Chaffles loaded up with marshmallows sit for some time until you set up your chocolate ganache.

7. Either in an Instant Pot or Double Boiler, dissolve Sugar-Free Chocolate along with Cocoa Butter until completely liquefied.

8. Take every Sweet Chaffle loaded up with Marshmallow and dunk into the Chocolate around the entire trip covering the entirety of the marshmallows.

9. Allow it to sit on a rack until completely dry.

NUTRITIONAL INFORMATION:

- 3 Big Smores, each with 368 Calories, 3g of Carbohydrates, 8g of Fiber, 11g of Protein, and 23g of Fat.

Breakfast Chaffle Sandwich

Servings: 1 Cooking time: 10 minutes

INGREDIENTS

- 2 basics of cooked chaffles
- Baking spray
- 2 slices of bacon
- 1 egg

TRAVEL DIRECTIONS

1. Spray oil into your pan.
2. Place it on medium food.
3. Cook the bacon until golden and crispy.
4. Place the bacon on a chaffle.
5. In the same pan, cook the egg without mixing until the yolk is firm.
6. Add the egg on top of the bacon.
7. Top with another chaffle.

Nutritional Information:

- Calories 514 Total Fat 47g Saturated Fat 27g Cholesterol 274mg Sodium 565mg Potassium 106mg Total Carbohydrates 2g Dietary Fiber 1g Protein 21g Total Sugars 1g

Cookie Dough Chaffle

Servings: 4 Cooking time: 7-9 minutes

INGREDIENTS

- Seizure
- 4 eg Gs
- ¼ cup of whipped cream
- 1 teaspoon of vanilla extract
- ¼ cup of stevia
- 6 tablespoons of coconut flour
- 1 teaspoon of baking powder
- Pinch of salt
- ¼ cup of unsweetened chocolate chips
- Others
- 2 tablespoons of cooking spray to brush the waffle iron
- ¼ cup of whipped cream, beaten

TRAVEL DIRECTIONS

1. Preheat the waffle iron.
2. Add the eggs and whipped cream to a bowl and stir in the vanilla extract, stevia, coconut flour, baking powder and salt. Mix until just combined.
3. Stir in the chocolate chips and combine.

4. Brush the heated water maker with cooking spray and add a few tablespoons of the batter.

5. Close the lid and cook for about 7-8 minutes, depending on yourwaffle iron.

6. Serve with whipped cream on top.

Nutritional Information:

- Calories 3, Fat 32.3g, Carbohydrates 12.6g, Sugar 0.5g, Protein 9g, Sodium 117mg

Thanksgiving Pumpkin Spice Chaffle

Servings: 4 Cooking time: 5 minutes

INGREDIENTS

- 1 cup of egg whites
- ¼ cup of pumpkin puree
- 2 teaspoons. pumpkin pie spice
- 2 teaspoons. coconut flour
- ½ tsp. vanilla
- 1 tsp. baking powder
- 1 tsp. baking powder
- 1/8 teaspoon of cinnamon powder
- 1 cup mozzarella cheese, grated
- 1/2 tsp. garlic powder

TRAVEL DIRECTIONS

1. Switch on your square waffle iron. Spray with nonstick cooking spray.
2. Beat the egg white with the whisk until light and white.
3. Add pumpkin puree, pump in pie spices , mix coconut flour into egg whites and beat again.

4. Stir in the cheese, cinnamon powder, garlic powder, baking powder and powder.
5. Pour ½ of the batter into the waffle iron.
6. Close the maker and cook for about 3 minutes.
7. Repeat with the remaining batter.
8. Remove chaffles from the maker.
9. Serve hot and enjoy!

Nutritional Information:
- Protein: 51% 66 kcal Fat: 41% 53 kcal Carbohydrates: 8% kcal

Pumpkin Spice Chaffles

Servings: 2 Cooking time: 14 minutes

INGREDIENTS

- 1 egg, beaten
- ½ teaspoon pumpkin pie spice
- ½ cup of finely grated mozzarella cheese
- 1 tbsp sugar-free pumpkin puree

TRAVEL DIRECTIONS

1. Preheat the waffle iron.
2. Combine all in a medium bowl.
3. Open the iron, pour half of the batter into it , cooking it and connect until it is crispy, 6 to 7 minutes.
4. Remove the chaffle to a plate and set aside.
5. Make another chaffle with the remaining batter.
6. Let cool and then serve.

Nutritional Information:

- Calories 90 Fat 6.46g Carbohydrates 1.98g Net Carbohydrates 1.58g Protein 5.94g

Keto Carnivore Waffle

Serving: 2 Cook time: 10 min

INGREDIENTS

- egg

- ½ cup ground pork rinds

- ⅓ cup mozzarella cheese

- A pinch of salt

TRAVEL DIRECTIONS

1. Firstly, preheat waffle maker to medium high heat.

2. Whisk together egg, cheese, ground pork rinds, and salt.

3. mixing carnivore waffle

4. Pour paffle mixture into the center of the waffle iron. Then close the waffle maker and let cook for 3-5 minutes or until waffle is golden brown and set.

5. adding carnivore waffle mixture to waffle iron

6. Then Remove paffle from the waffle maker and present.

Creamed Chipped Beef On Chaffle

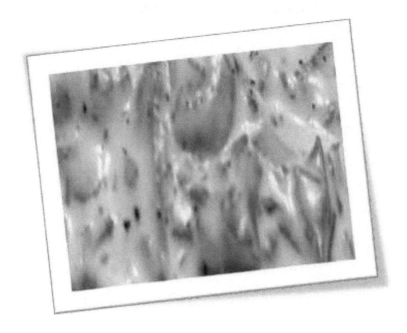

Servings: 8 Cook time: 20 min

INGREDIENTS

- 8 chaffles

- tbsp margarine or bacon oil

- 6 ounces dried meat cut into 3D squares

- 1/2 cup hamburger stock

- 8 ounces cream cheddar cubed

- 1/3 cup weighty cream

- dark pepper to taste

TRAVEL DIRECTIONS

1. Set up the chaffles as indicated by directions above. In the event that

you plan on serving promptly, keep the chaffles in the oven on warm while you make the creamed chipped hamburger.

2. Flush the hamburger in a bowl of warm water a couple of times to lessen pungency whenever wanted. 3D shapes the meat, at that point fry in a non-stick skillet in your fat of decision for 2-3 minutes.

3. Add the meat stock and stew for another 2-3 minutes, at that point add the cubed cream cheddar and substantial cream. Whisk continually until the cream cheddar disintegrates, around 3 minutes. Add pepper to taste and turn the heat down to stew while you finish your chaffles. In the event that the sauce is too thick, slim it with extra meat stock 2 tablespoons all at once until it arrives at your ideal consistency.

4. To serve, pour an inadequate 1/4 cup of creamed chipped hamburger more than one chaffle.

5. Macros per serving, not including the chaffles: 147 calories, 2 grams net carbs, 9 grams protein, 12 grams fat. Make a point to ascertain the macros for the chaffle formula you decide to utilize. In the event that you utilize the flavorful cheddar formula I gave in the notes above, it adds an extra 90 calories, 1 gram of net carbs, 7 grams of protein, and 7grams of fat.

Nutritional Information:

- Calories 666, Fat 55.2g, Carbohydrates 4.8g, Sugar 0.4g, Protein 37.5g, Sodium 235mg

Keto Sausage Omelet Chaffle

Serving: 3 Cook time: 12 min

INGREDIENTS

- 2 eggs
- tsp. diced tomato
- 1 tsp. diced onion
- 1 tsp. diced green peppers
- 1/4 cup finely shredded cheddar (your flavor decision)
- salt and pepper to taste
- 4 small wiener patties (or any meat of your decision)

DIRECTIONS:

1. Break eggs in a bowl or estimating cup and scramble well

2. Add salt and pepper flavors and blend well

3. Add tomato, green pepper, and onions and blend once more

4. Wrap up by adding shredded cheddar and blending till totally mixed

5. Pour 1/4 of hitter into smaller than normal waffle producer and permit to cook for 2-3 minutes (or somewhat more on the off chance that you like fresh)

6. Eliminate from waffle creator and rehash till every one of the 4 chafflesare done

7. Spot scaled down hotdog patties on chaffle (add fixings of your decision) and top with another chaffle

8. Enjoy!

Nutritional Information:

- YIELD: 4 chaffles SERVING SIZE: 2 chaffles
- Amount Per Serving: CALORIES: 173

Best Easy Keto Sloppy Joes

Servings: 4 Cook time: 10 min

INGREDIENTS

- lb ground hamburger
- 1/2 cup chopped green pepper
- 1 tsp garlic granules (or powder or new minced)
- 1 tsp onion powder
- 1/2 tsp dark pepper
- 1/2 tsp salt
- 1/8 tsp cayenne pepper (to 1/4 tsp relying upon zest inclination)
- 1 cup pureed tomatoes
- 1 tbsp apple juice vinegar

DIRECTIONS:

1. Brown the ground hamburger in a skillet on medium-high heat. As it browns, add the chopped green pepper to cook. Following 3-4 minutes,or once the meat is browned and peppers cooked, channel the

abundance fat.

2. Sprinkle on the garlic granules, onion powder, red pepper, dark pepper, and salt. Mix to join.

3. Add the pureed tomatoes and apple juice vinegar. Blend, at that point bring to a stew and turn the heat down to low. Stew for 5 to 10 minutes.

4. Serve alone or on keto bread, chaffles, or even zucchini noodles.

Nutritional Information:

- YIELD: 4 SERVING SIZE: 1/4 of recipe

- Amount Per Serving: CALORIES: 227TOTAL FAT: 12gSATURATED FAT: 5gTRANS FAT: 0gUNSATURATED FAT: 0g CHOLESTEROL

Chocolate Sandwich Chaffles

Servings: 2 Cooking time: 10 minutes

INGREDIENTS

- Chaffles
- 1 organic egg, beaten
- 1 ounce cream cheese, softened
- 2 tablespoons of almond flour
- 1 tablespoon of cocoa powder
- 2 teaspoons of erythritol
- 1 teaspoon of organic vanilla extract
- Stuffing
- 2 tablespoons cream cheese, softened
- 2 tablespoons of erythritol
- ½ tablespoon of cocoa powder
- ¼ teaspoon of organic vanilla extract

TRAVEL DIRECTIONS

1. Preheat a mini waffle iron and then grease it.

2. For chaffles: put all in a medium bowl and mix with a fork until well blended. Place half of the mixture in the preheated waffle iron and cook for about 3-5 minutes.

3. Repeat with the remaining mixture.

4. Meanwhile for filling: put all in a medium bowl and beat well with a hand mixer.

5. Serve each chaffle with chocolate mixture.

Nutritional information:

- Calories 192 Net carbohydrates: g Total fat 16 g Saturated fat 7.6 g Cholesterol 113 mg Sodium 115 mg Total carbohydrates 4.4 g Fiber 1.9 g Sugar 0.8 g Protein 5.7 g

Berry sauce Sandwich Chaffles

Servings: 2 Cooking time: 8 minutes

INGREDIENTS

- Stuffing
- 3 ounces of frozen mixed berries, thawed with the juice
- 1 tablespoon of erythritol
- 1 tablespoon of water
- ¼ tablespoon of fresh lemon juice
- 2 teaspoons of cream
- Chaffles
- 1 large organic egg , beaten
- ½ cup of cheddar cheese, shredded
- 2 tablespoons of almond flour

TRAVEL DIRECTIONS

1. For berry sauce: In a saucepan, add the berries, erythritol, water and lemon juice over medium heat and cook for about 8– minutes, pressing down occasionally with a spoon.

2. Remove the saucepan from the heat and let it cool before serving.

3. Preheat and grease a mini-iron.

4. In a bowl, add the egg, cheddar cheese and almond flour and beat until well blended. Place half of the mixture in a preheated waffle iron and cook for about 3-5 minutes.

5. Repeat with the remaining mixture.

6. Serve each husk with cream and berry sauce.

Nutritional information:

- Calories 222 Net carbohydrates 4 g Total fat 16 g Saturated fat 7.2 g Cholesterol 123 mg Sodium 212 mg Total carbohydrates 7 g Fiber 2.3 g Sugar 3.8 g Protein 10.5 g

Pork Sandwich Chaffles

Servings: 4 Preparation time: 16 minu tes

INGREDIENTS

- Chaffles
- 2 large organic eggs
- ¼ cup of super fine blanched almond flour
- ¾ teaspoon of organic baking powder
- ½ teaspoon of garlic powder
- 1 cup of cheddar cheese, shredded
- Stuffing
- 12 ounces of cooked pork, sliced
- 1 tomato, sliced
- 4 salad leaves

TRAVEL DIRECTIONS

1. Preheat a mini waffle iron and then grease it.
2. For chaffles: In a bowl, add the eggs, almond flour, baking powder and garlic powder and beat until well blended.
3. Add the cheese and stir to combine.
4. Put ¼ of the mixture in the preheated waffle iron and cook for about 3 minutes.

5. Repeat with the remaining mixture.
6. Serve each chaffle with filling

Nutritional information:

- Calories 319 Net carbohydrates 2.5 g Total fat 18.2 g Saturated fat 8 g Cholesterol 185 mg Sodium 263 mg Total carbohydrates 3.5 g Fiber 1 g Sugar 0.9 g Protein 34.2 g

Tomato sandwich Chaffles

Servings: 2 Cooking time: 6 minutes

INGREDIENTS

- Chaffles
- 1 large organic egg, beaten
- ½ cup of colby jack cheese, chopped
- 1/8 teaspoon organic vanilla extract
- Stuffing
- 1 small tomato, sliced
- 2 teaspoons of fresh basil leaves

TRAVEL DIRECTIONS

1. Preheat a mini waffle iron and then grease it.
2. For chaffles: put all in a small bowl and stir to combine.
3. Put half of the mixture in the preheated waffle iron and cook for about minutes.
4. Repeat with the remaining mixture.
5. Serve each chaffle with tomato slices and basil leaves.

Nutritional information:

- Calories 155 Net carbohydrates 2.4 g Total fat 11 g Saturated fat 6.8 g Cholesterol 118 mg Sodium 217 mg Total carbohydrates 3 g Fiber 0.6 g Sugar 1.4 g Protein 9.6 g

Seafood Chaffles

Servings: 6 Cooking time: 25 minutes

INGREDIENTS

- 1 pound of crabmeat
- 1/3 cup of Panko breadcrumbs
- 1 egg
- 2 tablespoons of thick Greek yogurt
- 1 teaspoon of Dijon mustard
- 2 tbsp parsley and chives, fresh
- 1 teaspoon of Italian herbs
- 1 lemon, squeezed

TRAVEL DIRECTIONS

- Salt, pepper to taste
- Add the meat. Mix well.
- Shape the mixture into round patties.
- Cook 1 patty for 3 minutes.
- Remove it and repeat the process with the remaining crab chaff mixture.
- Once done, remove and enjoy warm.

Nutritional Information:

- Calories per serving: 99 Kcal ; Fat: 8 g ; Carbohydrates: 4 g ; Protein: 16 g

Western Bacon Cheeseburger Chaffle Recipe

Servings: 3 Cook time: 10 min

INGREDIENTS

- Basic Chaffle Recipe
- 1/2 Lb Ground Beef Hamburger Patty (Note 1)
- 1 Slice Cheddar Cheese
- Tbsp Sugar Free Barbecue Sauce (Note 2)
- Strips Sugar Free Bacon
- 1 Serving Keto Airfryer Onion Rings (Note 3)

INSTRUCTIONS

1. Start the onion rings formula and keep on venturing two once they're inthe AirFryer.

2. While the onion rings are preparing, cook the two chaffles and put in a safe spot. Cover to keep warm.

3. Cook the bacon using your favored cooking strategy (oven/microwave/burner). We like to keep it straightforward by popping them in the microwave, covered, for around 2-3 minutes (contingent upon how fresh you like it and the brand). When cooked, move to a paper towel lined plate and put in a safe spot.

4. Cook the burger patty using your favored cooking strategy (barbecue/burner/oven). We lean toward the barbecue - high heat, approx. 5 minutes for every side until 160 degrees (medium).

5. Just prior to eliminating your cheeseburger from its heat source, top with a cut of cheddar. Keep set up for around 1 moment to soften the cheddar.

6. Fabricate your Hamburger - place the cheeseburger patty on one chaffle and top with the bacon, onion rings and grill sauce. Spot the second chaffle on top and enjoy right away.

Nutritional information:

- Calories 248 Net carbohydrates 1.2 g Total fat 24.3 g Saturated fat 4.9 g

Keto Fried Fish Sandwich

Servings: 3 Cook time: 30 min

INGREDIENTS

- Keto Fried Fish
- 16 ounces white fish cut into 3 pieces
- 1/2 cup almond flour
- 1/2 cup shredded parmesan cheddar
- 1/2 teaspoon garlic powder
- 1/2 teaspoon salt
- 1/2 teaspoon dark pepper
- egg
- Garlic Cheddar Biscuits
- 4 eggs
- cups shredded cheddar
- 1 teaspoon garlic powder
- Keto Fish Sandwich garnishes
- cuts American cheddar

- tablespoons tartar sauce
- Lettuce (discretionary)
- Tomato Slices (discretionary)

INSTRUCTION:

1. Pour your oil in an enormous cast iron skillet or a profound fryer and heat the oil to 350ºF.
2. Cut your fish so they are around 4 inch wide.
3. In a shallow bowl or pie plate join the almond flour, cheddar, galic, saltand pepper.
4. In another shallow bowl or pie plate, whisk the egg until its joined.
5. Dunk the fish into the egg then into the almond flour blend until very much covered.
6. Spot into the oil and cook for 2-3 minutes until the base is brilliant brown, flip and cook for another 2-3 minutes until brilliant brown and cooked through. Spot on a chilling rack to trickle overabundance oil. Rehash with different bits of fish ensuring you dont over swarm the container.
7. While you cook your fish heat up your scramble scaled down waffle creator.
8. In a little bowl blend the egg, garlic powder, and shredded cheddar.
9. When the scramble waffle producer is heated up include 1/sixth the chaffle combination. Cook for 4 minutes and eliminate. Rehash this progression with the chaffle blend.
10. Spot the fish ontop of a chaffle top with a cut of cheddar and one tablespoon of tarter sauce, at that point top with another chaffle.

NUTRITION INFORMATION:

- Amount Per Serving: CALORIES: 600TOTAL FAT: 36gSATURATED FAT: 17gTRANS FAT: 1gCARBOHYDRATES: 5gNET CARBOHYDRATES: 4gFIBER: 1gSUGAR: 1gPROTEIN: 56g

Crab Rangoon Chaffle With Sweet Chili

Servings:4 Cook time: 10 min

INGREDIENTS

- Keto Fried Fish
- 16 ounces white fish cut into 3 pieces
- 1/2 cup almond flour
- 1/2 cup shredded parmesan cheddar
- 1/2 teaspoon garlic powder
- 1/2 teaspoon salt
- 1/2 teaspoon dark pepper
- egg
- Garlic Cheddar Biscuits
- 4 eggs
- cups shredded cheddar
- 1 teaspoon garlic powder
- Keto Fish Sandwich garnishes
- cuts American cheddar
- tablespoons tarter sauce

- Lettuce (discretionary)
- Tomato Slices (discretionary)

GUIDELINES

1. Pour your oil in an enormous cast iron skillet or a profound fryer and heat the oil to 350ºF.
2. Cut your fish so they are around 4 inch wide.
3. In a shallow bowl or pie plate join the almond flour, cheddar, galic, saltand pepper.
4. In another shallow bowl or pie plate, whisk the egg until its joined.
5. Dunk the fish into the egg then into the almond flour blend until very much covered.
6. Spot into the oil and cook for 2-3 minutes until the base is brilliant brown, flip and cook for another 2-3 minutes until brilliant brown and cooked through. Spot on a chilling rack to trickle overabundance oil. Rehash with different bits of fish ensuring you dont over swarm the container.
7. While you cook your fish heat up your scramble scaled down waffle creator.
8. In a little bowl blend the egg, garlic powder, and shredded cheddar.
9. When the scramble waffle producer is heated up include 1/sixth the chaffle combination. Cook for 4 minutes and eliminate. Rehash this progression with the chaffle blend.
10. Spot the fish ontop of a chaffle top with a cut of cheddar and one tablespoon of tartar sauce, at that point top with another chaffle.

NUTRITION Information:
- Serving: 2chafflesCalories: 349kcalCarbohydrates: 3gProtein: 30gFat: 23gSaturated Fat: 13gTrans
  Fat: 1gCholesterol: 240mgSodium: 794mgPotassium: 347mgFiber: 1gSugar: 1g

Rye Bread Chaffle

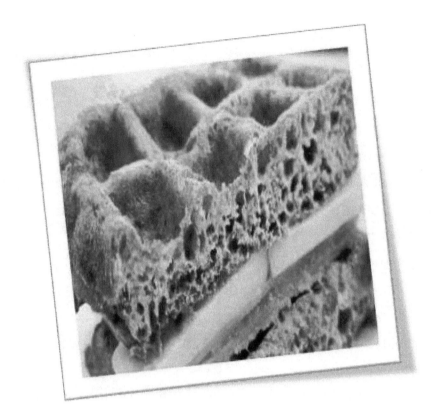

Servings: 1 Cook time: 10 min

INGREDIENTS

- 1/2 cup shredded mozzarella
- TB pecan flour
- 1 TB pork rind crumbs
- 1/4 tsp baking powder
- 1 large egg
- 1 TB rye sourdough starter (see video)
- 1/2 TB brown mustard

DIRECTIONS

Join mozzarella, walnut flour, pork skin morsels and heating powder. For the best surface, do this in a food processor and heartbeat 7-8 times until your dryseem as though bread morsels.

Add the egg, rye sourdough starter (see the video on the best way to make this) and the brown mustard. Blend or cycle until you have a for the most partsmooth hitter.

Sprinkle in the caraway seeds and blend or heartbeat momentarily to fuse. Cook the hitter in a waffle producer until you at this point don't see steam coming out (around 5 minutes). You will have sufficient hitter to fill two Dash Minis (with somewhat left finished) or two square waffles in a Dash NoMess. In the event that you twofold the formula, it fills a Dash No Mess consummately.

Nutrition Information:

- 3g net carbs each

Keto Protein Chaffle

Servings: 1 Cooking time: 8 minutes

INGREDIENTS

- 1 egg (beaten)
- ½ cup of whey protein powder
- A pinch of salt
- 1 tsp baking powder
- 3 tbsp sour cream
- ½ teaspoon of vanilla extract
- Topping:
- 2 tablespoons of whipped cream
- 1 tbsp granulated excursion

TRAVEL DIRECTIONS

1. Pick the waffle iron to preheat it and spray it with a non-stick cooking spray.
2. Beat the egg, vanilla and sour cream in a mixing bowl.
3. In another mixing bowl, combine the egg white powder, baking powder and salt.

4. Pour the flour mixture into the mixture and mix until the are wellblended and you form a smooth batter.

5. Pour an appropriate amount of the batter into the waffle iron and spread the batter up to the edges to cover all the holes in the waffle iron.

6. Close the waffle iron and cook for about 4 minutes or according to the settings of your waffle iron.

7. After the cooking cycle, use a plastic or silicone utensil to remove the chaffle from the waffle iron.

8. Repeat steps 4 to 6 until you have cooked all the batter in chaff.

9. Beat for the topping, the room by each other and rotate in a mixing bowl to a smooth and fluffy.

10.   Cover the chaffles with the cream and enjoy.

Nutritional Information:

- Fat 25.9g 33% Carbohydrates 13.1g 5% Sugars 2.1g Protein 41.6g

Chaffle Tacos

Servings: 4 Cooking time: 15 minutes

INGREDIENTS

- Chaffle:
- 2 tbsp coconut flour
- 3 eggs (beaten)
- ½ cup of grated mozzarella cheese
- ½ cup of shredded cheddar cheese
- A pinch of salt
- ½ teaspoon of oregano
- Taco filling:
- 1 clove of garlic (finely chopped)
- 1 small onion (finely chopped)
- ½ pound ground beef
- 1 tsp olive oil
- 1 teaspoon of cumin
- ½ tsp Italian herbs
- 1 tsp paprika powder
- 1 teaspoon chili powder
- 1 roma tomato (diced)
- 1 green pepper (diced)

- 4 tablespoons of our cream
- 1 tbsp chopped green onions

TRAVEL DIRECTIONS

1. Plug in the waffle iron to preheat it and spray it with nonstick cooking spray.
2. In a mixing bowl, combine the mozzarella cheese, cheddar, coconut flour, salt and oregano. Add the eggs and mix until the are well blended.
3. Fill the waffle iron with an appropriate amount of the batter. Spread the batter up to the edges to cover the entire hole in the waffle iron.
4. Close the waffle iron and cook for about 5 minutes or according to the settings of the waffle iron.
5. After the cooking cycle, use a plastic or silicone utensil to remove the chaff from the waffle iron. Put aside.
6. Repeat steps 3 to 5 until you have cooked all the batter in chaff.
7. Heat a large skillet over medium to high heat.
8. Add the ground beef and fry until brown, breaking apart while sautéing. Place the meat on a paper towel-lined plate to drain and wipe the pan clean.
9. Add the olive oil and let it heat up.
10. Add the onions and garlic and sauté for 3-4 minutes or until the onion is translucent, stirring often.
11. Add the diced tomatoes and green pepper. Boil for 1 minute.
12. Add the browned ground beef. Stir in the cumin, paprika, chili powder and Italian herbs.
13. Reduce heat and cook on low heat for about 8 minutes, stirring frequently to prevent burning.
14. Remove the pan from the heat.
15. Spoon the taco mixture into the chaffles and top with chopped green onion and sour cream.
16. To enjoy.

Nutritional information:

- Fat 5 g 22% Carbohydrates 12.6 g of 5% Sugars 4.5 g P roteïne 28.6 g

Chaffle With Sausage Gravy

Servings: 2 Cooking time: 15 minutes

INGREDIENTS

- Sausage gravy:
- ¼ cup of cooked breakfast sausage
- 1/8 teaspoon of onion powder
- 1/8 teaspoon of garlic powder
- ½ teaspoon of pepper or more to taste
- 3 tbsp chicken stock
- 2 tsp cream cheese
- 2 tbsp heavy whipping cream
- ¼ teaspoon of oregano
- Chaffle:
- 1 tbsp almond flour
- 1 tbsp finely chopped onion
- 1/8 teaspoon of salt
- ¼ tsp baking powder
- ½ cup of mozzarella cheese

- 1 egg (beaten)

TRAVEL DIRECTIONS

1. Plug in the waffle iron to preheat it and spray it with nonstick cooking spray.
2. In a mixing bowl, combine the almond flour, chopped onion, mozzarella, baking powder and salt. Add the egg and mix until the are well blended.
3. Fill the waffle iron with ½ of the batter and spread the batter up to the edges to cover all the holes in the waffle iron.
4. Close the waffle iron and bake for about minutes or according to the waffle iron settings.
5. After the baking cycle, remove the chaffle from the waffle iron with a silicone or plastic utensil.
6. Repeat at steps 3 through 5 until you have cooked all the batter in chaff.
7. Heat a skillet over medium to high heat. Add cooked sausage and sear until sausage is brown, stirring often to avoid burning.
8. Pour in the chicken stock and add the oregano, garlic powder, onion powder, pepper, cream cheese and whipped cream.
9. Bring to a boil, reduce heat and simmer for about 7 minutes or until gravy thickens.
10. Serve the chaffles with the gravy and enjoy.

Nutritional Information:

- Fat 16.6g 21% Carbohydrates 3.3g 1% Sugars 0.7g Protein 9.8g

Save Chaffle Sandwich

Servings: 2 Cooking time: 5 minutes

INGREDIENTS

- 1 large egg
- 1 tbsp. almond flour
- 1 tbsp. full-fat Greek yogurt
- 1/8 teaspoon of baking powder
- 1/4 cup of grated Swiss cheese
- 4 salad leaves

TRAVEL DIRECTIONS

1. Turn on your waffle iron.
2. Grease it with cooking spray.
3. Combine egg, almond flour, yogurt, baking powder and cheese in the mixing bowl.

4. Pour 1/2 cup of the batter into the center of your waffle iron and close the lid.

5. Cook chaffles for about 2-3 minutes until tender.

6. Repeat with the remaining batter

7. Once cooked, carefully transfer it to the plate. Serve salad leavesbetween 2 chaffles.

8. To enjoy!

Nutritional Information:
- Protein: 22% 40 kcal Fat: 66% 120 kcal Carbohydrates: 12% 22 kcal

Strawberry Shortcake Chaffle

Servings: 2 Cooking time: 8 minutes

INGREDIENTS

- ½ teaspoon of cinnamon
- ½ cup of grated mozzarella cheese
- 1 tsp sugar-free maple syrup
- 2 tsp granulated swerve
- 1 egg (beaten)
- 1 tbsp almond flour
- Topping:
- 3 fresh strawberries (sliced)
- 2 tsp granulated swerve
- 1 tablespoon of whipped cream
- ¼ teaspoon of vanilla extract
- 4 tbsp cream cheese (softened)

TRAVEL DIRECTIONS

1. Plug in the waffle iron to preheat it and spray it with nonstick cooking spray.

2. Mix in a bowl the cinnamon, swerve, cheese and almond flour. Add the egg and maple syrup. Mix until are well combined.

3. Pour an appropriate amount of the batter in the waffle iron and divide the batter to the edges to all the holes of the waffle iron to be covered.

4. Close the waffle iron and cook for about minutes or according tothe settings of your waffle iron.

5. After the cooking cycle, remove the chimney from the waffle iron with a plastic or silicone utensil.

6. Repeat steps 3 through 5 until you have cooked all the batter to chaff.

7. For the topping, mix the cream cheese, vanilla and whipped cream in a mixing bowl. Beat until the mixture is smooth and fluffy.

8. Cover the chaffles with the cream and the sliced strawberries.

9. Serve and enjoy .

Nutritional Information:

- Fat 15g 19% Carbohydrates **5.2g** 2% Sugars 1.3g Protein 7.3g

Cocoa Chaffles With Coconut Cream

Servings: 2 Cooking time: 5 minutes

INGREDIENTS

- 1 egg
- 1/2 cup of mozzarella cheese
- 1 teaspoon of stevia
- 1 teaspoon of vanilla
- 2 tablespoons. almon d flower
- 1 tbsp. sugar-free chocolate chips
- 2 tablespoons. cocoa powder
- TOPPING
- 1 scoop of coconut cream
- 1 tbsp. coconut flour

TRAVEL DIRECTIONS

1. Combine the chaffle in a bowl and mix well.
2. Preheat your dashmini waffle iron. Spray waffle iron with cooking spray.
3. Pour 1/2 batter into the minute waffle iron and close the lid.

4. Bake chaffles for about 2 minutes and remove them from the maker.
5. Make chaffles from the rest of the batter.
6. Serve with a scoop of coconut cream between two husks.
7. Drizzle coconut flour over it.
8. Enjoy with afternoon coffee!

Nutritional Information:
- Protein: 26% 60 kcal Fat: 65% 152 kcal Carbohydrates: 21 kcal

Conclusion

I hope all of you loved tasty chaffles recipes.We all love chaffles because they're supplement thick, produced using two ingredients (or more whenever wanted) and excessively quick to assemble and cook — and even for one individual.

Chaffles can be made with any sort of ground cheddar. The high flour content in waffles adds a lot of carbohydrates, making them unhealthy according to the recommendations of the keto diet. Chaffles, on the other hand, have no flour. Added ingredients can change the surface marginally; however, the fundamental recipe has only two ingredients! We've found that extra flour of some kind makes chaffles shockingly better.

Anything from nut flour, coconut flour or psyllium husk powder can be utilized to make the chaffle surface awesome. The chaffle recipes are amazingly delectable. You will not understand that what you are really eating are cheesy eggs or cheesy waffles. A big advantage of chaffles is that they can be stored i.e frozen and you can reheat them in a toaster, skillet or conventional oven before eating them.

You can also microwave for 30 to 60 seconds. There are many chaffle recipes out there, so you'll never run out of an option that you need to set one up. There are even cheddar free covers for the individuals who need to maintain a strategic distance from or limit the intake of ground cheese.Try these delicious recipes and home and appreciate along with your family members. Good luck!

Lightning Source UK Ltd.
Milton Keynes UK
UKHW050817220421
382425UK00005B/25

a

ABRSM

Theory of Music Exams

MODEL ANSWERS

GRADE 6

2010

Welcome to ABRSM's *Theory of Music Exams Model Answers*, Grade 6, 2010. These answers are a useful resource for pupils and teachers preparing for ABRSM theory exams and should be used alongside the relevant published theory exam papers.

All the answers in this booklet would receive full marks but not all possible answers have been included for practicable reasons. In these cases other reasonable alternatives may also be awarded full marks. For composition-style questions only one example of the many possible answers is given.

For more information on how theory papers are marked and some general advice on taking theory exams, please refer to the booklet *These Music Exams* by Clara Taylor, which is available free of charge and can be downloaded from www.abrsm.org.

Using these answers

- Answers are given in the same order and, where possible, in the same layout as in the exam papers, making it easy to match answer to question.

- Where it is necessary to show the answer on a stave, the original stave is printed in grey with the answer shown in black, for example:

- Alternative answers are separated by an oblique stroke (/) or by *or*, for example:

    detached / bouncing the bow

- American note names, for example half note and quarter note, are accepted but have not been included in the answers as they are not used in the exam papers.

- Where the source is not identified in full in the question paper, the source information is given at the start of the answer to enable candidates to consult the original. Note that the specimen answers do not necessarily follow the composer's original.

- Extended roman numerals are used in answers that require chord identification. Full marks will also be awarded if basic roman is used in this type of question, provided major, minor, augmented or diminished is stated.